ALLUVIAL CITIES

Christopher M. Hannan

Texas Review Press
Huntsville, Texas

FIRST EDITION

Requests for permission to acknowledge material from this work should be sent to:

Permissions
    Texas Review Press
    English Department
    Sam Houston State University
    Huntsville, TX 77341-2146

Acknowledgments:

The Classical Outlook, "The Minoans of Angola"
Connecticut Review, "Ichthus"
The Double Dealer, "Epithalamion"
Louisiana Cultural Vistas, "The Nephilim" (Parts II-V)
The Southern Poetry Anthology, Volume IV: Louisiana, "Acquamorta"
The Texas Review, "The Nephilim" (Parts I & II)
Town Creek Poetry, "Pasta Milanese"
Quartet: Selected Poems from the Editors of Batture Willow Press, "The Nephilim," "Epithalamion," "Pasta Milanese," "The Minoans of Angola," "Acquamorta," "Ichthus," "Teaching My Wife to Peel Garlic," "Vespers"
New Orleans Review, "Salt Water Intrusion" (Parts 1 & 2)
Sliver of Stone, "Leadbelly," "Elephant Graves"
The Legal Studies Forum, "Pasta Milanese"

Library of Congress Cataloging-in-Publication Data

Hannan, Chris (Christopher M.) author.
  [Poems. Selections]
  Alluvial cities / Christopher M. Hannan. -- First edition.
      pages cm
  ISBN 978-1-68003-022-8 (pbk. : alk. paper)
  1. Small cities--Louisiana--Poetry. 2. Fishing villages--Louisiana--Poetry. 3. Louisiana--Poetry.
I. Title.
  PS3608.A715736A6 2015
  811'.6--dc23
                            2015003439

For Emily, Jack William, and Lila Rose,
all the Hannans and DiMarcos,
and for John Freeman

Contents

PART 1—ALLUVIAL CITIES

SALT WATER INTRUSION

For Ed, Junior, Pete and Dan – 2005

1. Breton Island, 1939

Fifty-five years ago, when the water in Half Moon Bay was still sweet
and the grass grew nearly all the way out to Bay Eloi,
Pete and me would hunt rabbits on the island.

> I know my way around curves in the dark of three AM,
> through Bayou Terre Aux Boeufs to Black Bay, how to slide in gaps
> between shoals of oysters, feel my way through knees
> of cypresses, till I reach the opening
> of Breton Sound, dark as my black hairs and thick
> with spring tides. We bounce in a lake skiff, Pete and me,
> twenty miles south-southeast to Breton Island,
> twenty-gauge barrels broke down in our laps.
>
> We beach the boat and mount the ancient silt
> where black mangroves and wax myrtles stand
> taut as our young skin and butch-waxed hair.
> There's more tail shaking these bushes than the houses on Conti.
> I light a smoke and pull on Pete's bourbon.
> The shotgun swings between my knees
> and I can almost feel the choke explode
> at the thought: I'll shoot every rabbit I see.
>
> Out here the brackish marsh turns briny
> like perfumed skin sweats when you rub it.
> The barrier islands swell at the Gulf's touch
> as salt currents swirl and rush
> into the body of the sound. Out here
> you smell the fertile mud mix with salt,
> the way you'd think the First Day smelled.
>
> In the dark I breathe out over the waters of Bay Eloi,
> until the sun bursts from the marsh.
> The morning is a good one to be twenty,
> walking through spartina grass to flush rabbits.

These days, you can't hardly find where Breton Island's at.
The Gulf and storms have chewed it all to hell,
and the deep-draught ships have eaten away the old marsh.

2. Mississippi River Gulf Outlet, 1958

They dug the MRGO in 1958, right through the heart of Alluvial City,
Hopedale and Shell Beach.

Down Florissant Highway me and my son bounce
through cypress groves and water oaks,
past St. Bernard Cemetery, old as dirt,
to Bayou La Loutre. They've already cut the road
past Blackie Campo's dock. Years ago I fished
with a cane pole and a spark-plug off the asphalt
that now is scree along this new canal's banks.
They'll dig all the way from Breton Sound
to the pontoon bridge at Paris Road.

The dragline chews through mud like a catfish
and flips to spit the spoil on the banks.
The boy asks why it stinks so bad.
I tell him it's because things die to feed
the oyster grass and Roseau canes,
and it's the smell of death that makes all
the redfish, trout, and flounder live in the marsh.
He barely hears, runs and jumps feet-first
into the sludge, giggling waist-deep in the earth.

Along the channel's shore the mud slides
like the flesh piled around my gut and cheeks,
once packed as firm as levee dirt.
These mounds will sag more with every day
they dig the outlet further toward the river
and let the Gulf seep inside these brackish bays.
The salt will kill the cypresses and lilies,
turn the banks hard as smokers' veins.
I cough and taste its tide deep in my lungs.

Last week I broke a loaf of St. Joseph's bread
and tossed the pieces out in our front yard
to keep our new house safe and ward off storms.
I don't know what's in the earth that does it,
makes loaves become the father of God,
and brings old men to see themselves erode in mud
while young ones fling themselves in it for fun.
By now the boy is covered head to toe,
and I can feel the dug mud in my gut.

I hose him off as best I can, and he laughs:
the mud smells of trout he'll catch some day.
I see the way of flesh as it pools at my feet.

They dug the channel to be 36 feet deep and 250 wide.
Now I'm eighty, and its eroded 2000 feet across,
sloughed off more with every passing hull.

3. Hurricane Betsy, 1965

Betsy blew through here in '65.

I don't know why they give storms women's names.
That counter-clockwise motion must be male;
they strengthen in warm waters when they're young.
It would be the womb, not the eye,
that held together female hurricanes;
but men trust in their eyes to keep them safe.
They spin themselves against time till the end,
then weaken -- eye walls collapse, circulation slows,
and they pour their dying rage into broken earth.

The shift foreman can kiss my high dry ass:
he can stay at work and drown for all I care.
I take my wife and boys to her folks' house
behind the levee in Old Arabi
where the ground is high. We take what we can—
wedding pictures, birth certificates, favorite toys,
proof that we have set foot on the earth.

The floods came at night through Bayou Bienvenue,
where sheer winds whipped the surge up the Ship Channel.*
Gulf water forced itself into the marsh
and broke grass ridges like a rutting drunk.
Chalmette and all of St. Bernard had eight feet in the streets,
no levees to keep back those salty tides.
My wife can taste them in her tears
while the boys splash in what was our kitchen.
No one thought that new canal would ruin us.

I walk down the street to Pete's place;
he squats out front while his wife wails to God.
This is how St. Joseph would have felt at the cross,
no way to understand or make things better.
I wish I could have kept my sons from this,
risen like a barrier island to shield their youth.
But like Joseph, I am only flesh,
frail as maidencanes in a storm surge.
His bread must be drowned in my front yard.
Yet a counter-clockwise urge in me still spins:
I'll rebuild this goddamn house on salted earth.

---

*Another vernacular name for the MRGO.

My eye is focused where our mailbox still stands,
bearing my name; yet, I still choke back my salt.

Betsy pushed the Gulf up the Ship Channel
and over all of St. Bernard Parish.
The Corps hadn't thought of that
when they dug through the old marsh levees.

4. Erosion—December, 2005

Like worms, deep-draft ships have dug out the bottom,
eating away the sides with waves flung from their bows.
Now, thickened waters have scoured this Channel once again,
a clot bursting in breaches at the Arpent Canal levees,
hemorrhaging across the Parish, worse than Betsy.

For thirty years I've tried to get it closed,
this unnatural channel, eating its own banks.
I've watched it swallow islands wide as the memory
of days when I would run through Roseau canes
and chase the gallinules while daddy fished.
Now there's only cord-grass sparse as my grey hairs,
sterile mud where sea gulls peck. It has eroded
every day, vessels collapsing this man-made body
further into the thirty-six foot pit we can't control.

I don't get out that way much anymore.
My knees and back can't bounce like they used to,
hollow as old oaks on a cheniere
flooded by the wizening salty tides
of arthritis, emphysema, diabetes.
I'll take my grandkids fishing now and again,
but never too far past Hopedale Lagoon.
I don't like to see the land that's gone
like my old thighs, atrophied along the Channel.

They'll try to dam it off at the La Loutre Ridge,
dump riprap from the Long Rock jetties,
an embolism to hold back floods.
But me, I know it can't be closed;
salt will still leak through the arteries
of bayous that once bloomed with irises.

I can only cling to what little remains.
My sons think this has been my hobby, just to pass the time,
but they haven't watched this land decay.
What I once could swim across is now two thousand feet,
like the growing hole you feel when your wife gets buried
or when skin cancer sloughs off into your stomach.
Salt-burned grass can't hold soil loose as old bladders.
The rabbits won't return to Breton Island.

But the cypress knees still jut from Stump Lagoon,
and oyster beds are thick as my granddaughter's hair.
There's still freshwater in Bayou Terre Aux Boeufs,
though I feel salt water intrusion in my veins.

HOT WATER CANAL

In days of uncold blood the Sacred Heart
Brothers made St. Joseph's Feast a holiday.
March nineteenth, still too cold for swimming, we'd climb
into a flatboat, 45 Evinrude with a tiller.
A yank of the rope
turned over our throbbing outboard heart,
churned that cold darkness underneath
into a holy day of two-stroke exhaust—
bubbles in our prop wash,
chrism of oil halos popping all around
as we jumped into the Hot Water Canal.

Outfall from the Michoud plant
keeps the canal warm year round.
We'd launch the boat and cross the Bienvenue locks
to that hot water, where the first of us would slip out
with a plywood disc, shellacked as smooth as a relic,
sandpapered and planed in garages
where our fathers taught us carpentry.

Grab the rope, feet nailed down dead center,
and hold tight for the boat's lurch to lift you.
The trick is not to fall in where it's cold,
where the intracoastal barges push wakes
that gurgle and suck like fluid in your lungs.

Swing outside the wake at high tide
to feel the marsh cane brush your back and legs.
Forget the gnarled claws of crab traps and clamshells
sunk two feet below in rotten mud.
They'd strap flesh from bone like a scourge
and turn a plywood disc to a pine box.

But underneath those high March tides
dangers disappear like thoughts of tomorrow's
classes, far off as the dark bottom of the canal,
where wood and bone and holy days turn
to the oil in a two-stroke cycle of blood—
warm gasoline mixed with a viscous black.
It chokes out its flames and lubricates the veins
of an outboard engine till plaque gums the stator
and the heart dies that once
breathed a wake of holy spume.

THE NEPHILIM

— My Grandmother's Flooded House in Chalmette

So the Lord said, "I will wipe mankind, whom I have created, from the face of the earth — men and animals, and creatures that move along the ground, and birds of the air — for I am grieved that I have made them."

— Genesis 6:7

τέκνον ἐμόν, πῶς ἦλθες ὑπὸ ζόφον ἠερόεντα
ζωὸς ἐών; χαλεπὸν δὲ τάδε ζωοῖσιν ὁρᾶσθαι.
μέσσῳ γὰρ μεγάλοι ποταμοὶ καὶ δεινὰ ῥέεθρα . . .

My son, how did you come beneath this darkness
being still alive? It is hard for the living to see these places,
for between us and them there are great and terrible waters . . .

— Homer, Odyssey, Book XI, 155-58

I.   DEUCALIONIDS

The waters broke from the void before first light,
a divinity ripping through the trembling flesh
of marshes and the levees' old clay thighs,
covering every mile of St. Bernard Parish.

Houses with their cement slabs have floated
light as the rinds of watermelons you ate as a boy
and chucked into Lake Catherine, swelled to overflowing
by the god that surged into the Rigolets estuary

and left an afterbirth of sweet crude leaked
from foundered tanks. Cars hang like carrion
birds on the highest branches and torn roofs. Leached
of mud and flood waters, the houses we pass cry out

broken window panes, duct-taped fridges, and a stillness
that leaves us on the dead grass of this
woman's home, like so many thrown bones.

II.   DIAGENESIS

Dig deep enough, down through the earth,
past the mud and river silt and unglued carpet—
down through the deposits of old seawater,
fossilized hydrocarbons, dissolved furniture and drywall
and you may find the room your father
slept in as a boy. Further down, among the shades

that have rotted off the windows as if centuries
have passed, among the salt-burned photos
and the ectoplasm of oil sheens,
you will discover the face of your grandfather,
buried in 1965 just before Betsy, smiling
in the viscous trench you have dug to see what lies

in the muck. Along faults of waterlines
the walls have fractured, collapsing like shale
under the pressures of mold and sagging gypsum
board. The air is heavy, and the subterranean murk
pulsates a breathless heat in these final depths
of a long, humid summer. Turn the shovel again

and something glitters in the hole like pyrite—
a rosary, broken glass, pieces of your grandmother's
jewelry that she left behind in a box on the dresser,
and years' worth of Mardi Gras doubloons her children,
grandchildren, and great-grandchildren collected
on the corner of St. Charles and Polymnia, fused

tight as sandstone in their mildewed protective sheets.
Then, the shovel strikes the bedrock of the slab;
at the bottom, you glimpse your own face
next to your cousins' in an old Christmas picture,
decomposing among these layers of water and earth,
a geology that stratifies your gut, forms stones in your throat.

III.   KATABASIS

You must not remain too long in this place
where time does not move and the dead
clocks lie with the vastness of geological epochs,
their frozen faces ignorant of your presence,
gaping from the sludge that sucks the soles
of your boots, pulls you down, belching

as you balance to keep from falling into the black
alluvion. This is the archaeology of gutting
your grandmother's house, shoveling mud and leaked crude
left by the torrents that ripped through foundations
of levees, swallowed the marshes of your childhood
fishing spots, drowned the kitchen where your family

cooked on Christmas and Thanksgiving,
and washed over St. Mark's altar where they baptized
you and your sister. You gasp in the rank humidity,
disintegrated sheetrock, and mold as a stygian darkness
fills your lungs, and your feet sink further in the Acheron
that used to be the main hallway of this house.

You stumble through the strata of debris and memories, past
phantoms of half-buried clothes that clutch at your ankles,
your eyes watering as the Carnival doubloons flicker
in the ooze like coins in the mouths of the dead.
Struggling through the sediment, back towards the living
room, you reach the window where you first descended

into the house, and grasp the ledge to climb back into the daylight.
Your father and grandmother have been calling for you
to come out before darkness rises like a wraith and covers
the roads out of the desolation; but inside, you could not hear.
No echoes sound in the coagulated mire, only voices
that seem to whisper your name from the ground.

IV. NEKUIA

Before we can return home, through moldering shades we probe the dead
minnows decomposing in the bedroom, shards of windows
staring like lifeless eyes from the dimness, and the inescapable mud
that sticks thick as old blood to everything in the house, searching
for the wedding ring my grandmother left behind in the flood.

Below the oak-root bend of arthritic knuckles, she still bears
the mark, rubbed smooth as a river bed, of wearing for fifty years
this symbol of the man she loved, God, her family, and her home,
now lost among the remnants of rushing water and displaced earth.
It is the only thing she hopes to take away from this place.

From the door of the bedroom where her jewelry box disintegrated
in the rushing salt surge, we dig trenches one foot wide and deep,
carrying the shovelfuls of spoil – mixed with bits and pieces of her
clothes, earrings, shoes, and bed sheets – out to the front lawn.
With no running water, we sieve it all through a window screen,

pouring Diet Coke from the trunk of her flooded car into the mud
like a drink-offering of honey, milk, wine, and blood to the ghosts
that slowly reveal themselves, as the dirt washes away, in flashes
of silver and gold, speaking to us of past lives and the memories
welling in her eyes with every necklace and earring we unearth.

We grasp at these apparitions before they slip through our hands
and sink back into the blackness pooling like a Lethe below
the screen, where the Coke and sludge smell of asphodel.
As the light fades, we begin to lose hope of finding this one thing
she seeks in the destruction, that will bring her back to her life

before the flood. But then, the smiling curve of a plain gold ring
swims up through the fetid bilge, reflecting the house and the faces
of you, your father, and your cousins standing over the screen.
And as she slides it onto her hand, her eyes shine with thanks
and the streams of a different flood of salt no levees can contain.

V.   NOSTOS

Your father's boyhood home lies in ruins,
under the roof and rotted ceiling that sheltered him after his father died.
He returns with you once more—before the bulldozers come—to cut
       out pieces

of exposed rafters, ribs of old-growth pine
running red as marrow, smooth as bones, the length of the house.
These boards are heartwood, grown dense with time
and fifty years of holding back the rain: all eight-by-twos

with grains tight and strong as your grandmother's back
who raised five kids alone below these beams.
He will cut foot-long trivets for his family, relics
of this house, all the flood waters never reached.

Now, we will always have a foot in Zelda's kitchen.
He chooses a joist seasoned by oven smoke
and pot steam, the ruddy color of his skin,
with knots like his tears. He saws into the wood, choking:

You'll never find lumber like this again.

PART 2—TRINITIES

ARS

*— Poetry . . . is language that grows frequently incandescent,
giving off both light and heat.*
— Laurence Perrine and Thomas R. Arp,
Sound and Sense

A bonfire's parhelions,
embers burn heavenward
reflected in our

still gaze, axons
flaring the hermetic
darkness. The blaze

crackles as tongues
probe the black
sky like trochees

metering the night's
syntax. Our tinder —
branches, cones, fascicles

of loblolly pines —
kindled these flames
igniting the eigengrau

dark, where sparks
explode in iambic
bursts, burning bright

as the synaptic
flickers of nebulae,
when the medulla

of blackjack oak
and maple split
with heated sap.

These logs, metonyms
for bones burned
in our ancestors'

fires, make us
stare at dying
coals giving life

to this reaction
between carbon, oxygen
and a breath

of heat, illuminating
our small sphere,
until there remains

only charcoal, ash,
the glowing cinders,
these sundog syllables.

FATA MORGANA

Ever the dim beginning,
Ever the growth, the rounding of the circle,
Ever the summit and the merge at last, (to surely start again,)
Eidolons! eidolons!

— Walt Whitman, "Eidolons" from *Leaves of Grass*

Eastward, an eidolon
rises over unseen
waves, grayish protoplasm

barely felt beneath
our waking transom.
A form materializes,

the weird twilight
unshrouding an island
rookery of seabirds—

a ghost ship
on Black Bay,
appearing to scud

across the shoals
where breakers roll
like bow waves.

Among phantom sawgrass
masts, and hulls
of salted driftwood,

squawks rattle, morning's
incantations conjuring black
mangroves like specters

from the dawn.
The new-born roseate
spoonbills - pink spume

on half-lit sand—
mimic the guttural
chants of elders,

who raise blood-red
wings to dry
in murky light.

Vapors swirl leeward,
the water turning
warm, and brown

pelicans like shades
of daylight skimming
the lambent Gulf.

Our vision adjusts
as false dawn
illuminates the bay

over our hull's
rise and fall,
embodying the island —

a phantasm scuttled
under phosphorescent waves
reflecting the sunrise.

ΙΧΘΥΣ *

Shibboleths for communion
with what grows
in old mud,

oyster boats appear
to dredge dawn
from wet dark

earth. Those waking
lafitte skiffs intone
a murmured Matins,

the unseen revolutions
of diesel inboards,
as the sun

turns the sky
gray as oyster
flesh. The words,

crepuscular on sterns,
say *Miss Josephine*
or *Lady Alicia*.

You wonder why
the ancient rite
of giving names

to fishing boats
is not forgotten
like Latin mass.

It must be
that old belief
in the word

as man's sole
grasp on things
bigger than him.

---

*Pronounced "ichthus"; Homeric Greek for "fish," and Greek acrostic used by early Christians, combined with a fish symbol, for "Jesus Christ, God's Son, Savior."

A fish sign
at Pip's Dock
blinks *LIVE BAIT*

as you cross
the shell-paved lot.
Those oysters sound

like *Our Fathers*
chanted on Sunday:
words grown hard

and piled up
like oyster reefs
in brackish silt.

You know oysters
grasp something hard
as young spat

to grow shells,
and cling together
in the dark

mud for safety.
And you wonder
as sterns pass,

their names fading,
what the dredges
will drag up.

ΔΟΛΟΣ *

Treble hooks gleam
as you impale
a cocahoe's eyes

in nautical twilight
that lures you
past submerged forms

to unknown waters
where something stirs.
The angling sun

sinks, a rusty
Kahle hook barb
in your eyes.

The world reels
in your vision,
pierced by light.

A blind cast,
strain to see
your line's end.

As the bait
you feel struggling
to unhook itself

twitches, night ripples
like fin swirls
before a strike.

The line tightens;
you reel in
an empty hook.

So you run
a tense line
of thrashing wake,

---

*Pronounced "dolos"; Homeric Greek: "Trick" or "Fish Bait."

pulled by dying
light of day
that drags you

toward the dock.
You think *Can't*
get caught alone

in Black Bay,
darkness gaping westward,
about to swallow.

I SEE YOU BOYS OF SUMMER

I see you boys of summer in your ruin.
Man in his maggot's barren.
And boys are full and foreign to the pouch.
I am the man your father was.
We are the sons of flint and pitch.
O see the poles are kissing as they cross.

— Dylan Thomas

The gerrymandered sun
of June — Gulf
clouds barnstorm, dyed

dark and faux,
hiding white hair.
They make you

watch for rain
but you know
black-haired thunderheads

in waning afternoon
don't always keep
their slick promises.

Like all flesh
pressers, those billows
fake their shade.

Clouds can lie
that way forever;
but you age

towards the end
of dog days,
constituent of earth,

where you wane
and weaken under
politic June's manteau.

CAMINADA

Chenieres remember tides
in their duplicity:
the night-drawn tug

scours roots, drags
jetsam (day's empty
bottles, fish carcasses,

limbs, and skeletons
of crabtraps), forgotten
in the undercurrent's

ebbing. Saltwater drains
through silt sloughed
like yesterday past

live oak roots;
then, twisted sluggishly
as the dawn

eddies up, waking
like a pirogue,
slow as cormorants

ascending in darkness,
the inevitable turn
draws the deep

through the body
of Bay Desespere,
up the mouth

of Caminada Pass
over the cheniere.
Rising, the Gulf

chicanes like memory,
roots gripping dark,
formless, and submerged

earth for support
in ancient tides
that turn, always

washing the salt
over this island,
place of oaks.

L'HEURE BLEUE

It was evening all afternoon.

— Wallace Stevens,
"Thirteen Ways of Looking at a Blackbird, XIII"

Day's diapason tolls
in the mourning
doves' four notes,

arpeggiating as shadows
thicken beneath trees
and morning transitions

to midday. Diminished
movements of afternoon
hasten twilight, transpose

the muted sun
whose glare resolves
into these notes,

evening's prelude echoing
from an unseen
rhythm in limbs

before dark. Dusk
resonates like breath
before its last

chromatic strains fade,
red veins receding
among blue tones

the imperfect time
of night's reprise.
These last hours

resound with dying
light and song,
when darkness swells

around the shaded
and rattling throats
of evening doves.

ACQUAMORTA

Acqua chiusa, sonno delle paludi
che in larghe lamine maceri veleni,
ora bianca ora verde nei baleni,
*sei simile al mio cuore.**

— Salvatore Quasimodo, *Acquamorta*

The batture clings
around the knees
and gnarled limbs

of bald cypresses
and snagged driftwood
like old cartilage.

This soil lies
eroding as winter
currents stretch past

ligaments of levees.
Silt banks, sagging
as thighs, straddle

the fall's alluvion:
not quite earth
nor river's surge

but mud hovering
between the waters.
Eddies like gasps

reveal something unmoved
where the depths,
blood-thick with loam,

---

* *Closed water, dream of the swamps*
that in wide-hammered sheets steep poison,
now white, now green in the lightning,
you are like my heart.
-Author's translation

scour these shoals,
scleroses of tides
and riparian clay,

where you sink
ankle-deep and smell
the dusk quickening.

VESPERS

Night's mandibles gnaw
marrowed evening from
the fractured afternoon.

Cicadas rasp, rattling
lungs in air
coagulated with sweet-olive,

while day hemorrhages
its indigo veins
of sunlight staining

the bruised horizon.
Street lamps dilate,
your eyes adjusting

among shades conjured
from blood-red skies
and the deepening

dusk. The ascendant
moon hangs crescent
east of evening,

an ass's jawbone
swung through thousands
of dying days.

In your skin
throb the bites
of the night's

first mosquitoes. Cursing,
you crush them,
hands smearing blood

over welts rising
as the stars
begin to swell.

PART 3—ALTARS

From the collection "Tupa Tupa"

PASTA MILANESE

— or "Finnerchy"

ἀλλά μιν ἐξαπάτησεν ἐΰς πάις Ἰαπετοῖο
κλέψας ἀκαμάτοιο πυρὸς τηλέσκοπον. αὐγὴν
ἐν κοΐλῳ νάρθηκι

But the noble son of Iapetus outwitted him
and stole the far-seen gleam of unwearying fire
in a hollow fennel stalk

— Hesiod, *Theogony*

So much boils down to so little:
these fronds, glaucous green as the seas
behind your great grandmother's eyes,
their blooms spent in the ebbing winter,
will simmer with time and salted water
to almost nothing. She stirs the pot

in a rhythm of blood and foreign tongues,
breathing the steam of her ancestors' kitchens
that rises each March with Lenten vows —
the pungent smell of the slowly diminishing
greens, an essence of anise, and the memory
of picking *finnochi* for her *nonna's Milanese.*

Eighty years branch across her hands,
green stems grown from a chambered bulb
whose roots hold the soil of generations.
Far from their native Sicilian hills,
scattered in the grass of your aunts' and cousins'
yards, these hollow stalks still sprout

in fertile ground. She lowers the fire
hours later and empties the boiling stock
to strain all that is left of her
finnerchy, the fragrant "grass" in the family
recipe for St. Joseph's Day gravy.
Still, a deep bitterness will linger,

subtle as the hint of iron in church wine:
an earthy sting of licorice a lifetime
couldn't boil away. But she knows this flavor,
how to cover its starkness with touches of sugar
measured, like her rosaries, by muscle memory,
until she knows she's put in enough.

When everything begins to change
colors—the bright red of tomatoes
mellowing with onions to a claret brown
like rust or old blood—she will pour in her last
ingredients, the *con sarde* and *pignoli*,
and leave it all to cook on a low flame.

The gravy will thicken slowly as a dialect,
reducing in murmurs and muffled breaths
of steam, flavors blending beneath the surface
in a radiant heat that makes tongues
and mouths water in the heady aroma.
She sits, and the stove gleams like an altar

flickering under all she has prepared: candles
for *San Giuseppe*, stock pots for the pasta,
and a skillet where breadcrumbs becomes *mudrica*—
the Saint's sawdust—a transubstantiation
in sugar and oil on the fire she brings down
to keep it all from burning. This litany of seasonings

pervades the house with a reverence, and an incense
rises from the kitchen, redolent of cigarettes
and coffee, the brine of sardines, her perfume,
and the gravy that brings the family together
like a birth or a death, and fills your chest
with the sweet and forlorn scent of fennel.

PESCE ROSSO AL FORNO

-Baked Redfish

1.   *I Pescatori—The Fishers*

Long before the fasting days and ashes
and the midnight horses that stride Carnival's end,
before the memories of dust and the sacrifice of flesh
on Fridays, we will rise in the darkness that precedes
dawn to catch redfish for the St. Joseph's altar.

In these autumn months, down in the deepest reaches
of pipeline canals, they hover like echoes of a doxology,
barely moving in the stillness at the bottom,
feeding only on a running tide and clean water.
We will return to the old places where we know

there are oysterbeds that the bull reds haunt, trolling
for bait among the shells, an eternal hunger
drawing them back each year in a sacrament
to these same depths that have fed them for generations.
We follow the familiar routes we can't see

before sunrise, but discern by the contours
of the marsh, the floats of crab traps, and memory.
A Carolina rig with a sliding sinker,
an eighteen-inch leader, and a dead shrimp
will be our offerings to bring them to the surface—

these representations of Christ, his disciples, and the miraculous
loaves and fishes—placed on the altar as symbols
of what moves in unfathomed depths and reveals itself
only in the slight tugs and barely noticed ripples
trembling from the bottom in the uncertain moments

when something strikes. We cast into the silent, unmoving
darkness of the canal where the night's remnants reflect
the rising twilight, and in this rite of catching fish
for the St. Joseph's altar, our unspooling lines sing
the litany that wells in us each year, a running tide.

2.   *Il Sventrare—The Gutting*

In the sacral light of late Fall, with the old knives
and chopping board used only for cleaning fish,
we gut the day's catch in the yard, letting the blood
and slime wash onto the grass, a libation to the family
garden's eggplants, peppers, garlic, and tomatoes.

Rhythmic as a refrain, our hands open these bodies,
bronze-skin monstrances gleaming in the afternoon sun,
to remove the stomach, swim bladder, intestines,
and thick blood-lines that run along the bottom
of the fillets. We will fill them with the traditional

stuffing—breadcrumbs, hard-boiled eggs, onions—
and roast them whole, covered in lemon and olive oil,
the night before the feast. Until then, they will be frozen,
incorruptible as relics, martyrs awaiting apotheosis
in our family's kitchen, on the altar of St. Joseph.

3. Il Forno—The Oven

Bones season flesh with an ancestry of salt,
brackish stock rendered slowly into loins
along ribs and spine, the muscles' memory
of the sea. Lidless eyes reflect the flickering
fire that still burns in your great-grandmother's

O'Keefe and Merritt passed down to your father,
the deathless gaze of icons. Like phosphenes, the skin
glistens with a chrism of grease as the meat becomes
the white of eyes, proteins tightening under the old elements'
flames. Lemon and olive oil flow over

sides pierced to let the innermost parts
cook through, filling with the flavor of your mother's
seasonings. Underneath it all, tomatoes simmer
in a slow reduction that sweetens the bitterness
of citrus and softens the sting of the coarse black

pepper rubbed like myrrh on the fillets.
The head gapes from the lambent dark, bearing
up its hollowed remains around the backbone,
an axis that shapes the void to hold the simple
stuffing inside the body. This is how it begins

each year the night before the feast,
when we cook all the dishes to fill the Saint's table.
After everything is made, in the early dark
of late winter, the priest will bless the food,
sanctifying these generations-old

recipes. For now, the fish roasts in this cosmogony
of basic ingredients, creating the central course
for the altar from the raw and lifeless forms
of fin and tail as heat, simple flavors, and their tided
essences merge in the inherited tabernacle of the oven.

TEACHING MY WIFE TO PEEL GARLIC*

These toes are the print of the Devil's left foot,
sprouted where cloven soles fell on the earth
outside Eden's gates. The scarred mud gave root
to these curious softneck heads, the first herb
she helps me peel tonight to sauté in oil and butter.

Born of cursed earth, with skins thin as innocence,
these joined bits of flesh filled a raw world
with a pungence that sticks like salt to our hands
and makes our mouths water for the first savor
that cleansed the acid of apples from our lips.

Risen from ruined soil, this bulbous growth
wards off the evil eye and thwarts devourers of blood,
vampire, bacteria, or mosquito. An aphrodisiac, the stinking rose
strengthens the heart, quickens the thigh, and gives food
an essence that whets the tongue and lingers in pores.

With heat, the original sting of its taste will sweeten
to the subtle flavor you crave; but the sulphur of its genesis
hangs heavy on the breath. This seasoning made man
relish the fruits of the fallen world, tinged with bitterness
and sweat sown in the ground of his creation. Our recipe

calls for two cloves peeled, chopped, and simmered
to a sweat, until they turn translucent as wide eyes.
She wants to help, but uncertain what to do, she picks
the pieces cautiously and asks how to lay bare
the insides, to remove the leaf-thin veils that separate

us from these roots. Taking her hand, I teach her:
first, crush each clove beneath the flat of a knife
to loosen the skin and expose the naked flesh,
redolent of soil, and its bittersweet spice.
Next, finely chop. Then, our broken bits of garlic

---

*"When Satan stepped out of the Garden of Eden after the fall of man, garlic
sprang up from the spot where he placed his left foot and onion from that where
his right foot touched."
  — *Catholic Traditions in the Garden*, Ann Ball

will soften in the dark warmth of oil and butter
deepening the aroma in our nostrils, wetting our lips.
We'll savor this, though the smell will leak from our pores.
The scent will remind us of cooking tonight's recipe,
and how to get this earthy flesh separated
from its skin in the ancient rite of peeling garlic.

PART 4—HYMNS

Pelops, I will tell your story
differently from the men of old.

—PINDAR, *Olympian 1*, l. 36 (Nisetich, Trans.)

For so the Muse stood at my side
when I discovered this new mode of song.

—PINDAR, *Olympian 3*, l. 4 (Nisetich, Trans.)

I'm not sure, but I'm almost positive that all music in the world came
from New Orleans.

— ERNIE K-DOE, *Emperor of the Universe*

A Note On the Hymns

Growing up in New Orleans, I was surrounded by the rich musical heritage of the city and the region. A part of this musical culture that always intrigued me, even as a child, was the immense mythology of Louisiana music, peopled by characters such as John Henry, Stag O'Lee, and countless others. These mythic personalities remained with me throughout my youth and into college where I studied the Classics. The cultures of ancient Greece, Rome, and every other culturally advanced society that has left any record, exhibited highly developed mythologies used to explain external natural phenomena as well as the inner world of human experience.

At some point, I realized that the music I had grown up with and still listened to was the mythology of America, or at least the Deep South. All the characters whose stories were told over and over again by Leadbelly, Professor Longhair, and a myriad of others were simply reincarnations of the archetypes sung by Homer, Pindar, and Hesiod.

In the *Hymns* I have tried to connect ancient myth with these modern mythologies in poems that approximate the basic meters and rhyme schemes of the original songs. The use of song forms is meant to mimic the ancient tradition of adhering to established poetic/rhythmic forms while simultaneously reinterpreting well-known myths. The primary inspiration for this form comes from the ancient Epinecian odes of Pindar, choral songs composed in honor of victors in the sacred athletic contests of ancient Greece (i.e. the Olympic, Pythian, Nemean and Isthmian games). Pindar's highly idiosyncratic reinterpretation of older myths has been described as the "poetic expression of a preexisting fusion of . . . myths, where the earlier myth is officially subordinated to but acknowledged by the later myth." Gregory Nagy, PINDAR'S HOMER: THE LYRIC POSSESSION OF AN EPIC PAST (Johns Hopkins University Press, 1990). The *Hymns* in this book seek to continue this tradition of reinterpreting ancient myths and fusing them with their modern echoes in Louisiana's musical tradition.

TIPITINA*

-Henry Roland Byrd, aka Professor Longhair

Tipitina, tra la la la
Andera na ti na na
Tipitina oola mala walla dolla
Aeide tra la la.

Hey Luberta, oh Luberta
girl you hear me callin' you.
Come sing in me one time baby
like a muse is s'posed to do.

Say Luberta, whoa Luberta,
girl you tell me where you been.
Cause you're smellin' like a laurel
and talkin' Greek again.

You been hangin' on some others
in the groves of Helicon,
with them girls whose voices whisper
in ears of men they fall upon.

Leave Terpsichore to her dancin'
and Polymnia to her songs.
Let Thalia kiss them strangers
and you come on back home.

Swing your hips down off that mountain,
girl you know what we could do.
Leave them heights to Urania,
but take Erato's tricks with you.

I don't want those wine dark whispers
from the lips of Cálliōpe;
just bring your bourbon scented breathin'
back to my thirsty throat.

---

*There are nine streets in New Orleans named after the nine Greek muses. Their names in this poem are meant to be pronounced as their eponymous street names would be pronounced in the New Orleans vernacular.

Tell Eúterpe to keep her lipstick
and her rosy-fingered rouge.
You don't need no fancy painting
when you're with me bein' true.

Clio's had a slew of lovers
who I know put me to shame,
but I'm more lively than them others
who all lie in ancient graves.

And I don't want to feel the rhythms
from the tongue of Mélpōmene
cause every man she's touched got buried
once she came and made'em sing.

So Luberta, oh Luberta
girl you hear me callin' you
come down and help my singin'
'fore my song is ancient too.

JUNCO PARTNER

On down the road I come a stumblin',
Lawd, as loaded as Agave
followin' after Dionysus
and wobblin' all over the place.

I'd like to know what she was hittin'
when she ripped her boy apart
'cause that's the stuff I need to drink
to get me tore up like a god.

Stayin' seamless leaves you whole
like grapes still on the vine;
they won't split, they shrink and shrivel
becoming raisins like old men.

But gettin' ripped leaves you divided,
half mortal, half divine,
like a grape that's still a grape
when its dismembered into wine.

Dionysus was only human
when the Titans tore his limbs;
he had to get himself demolished
to drink nectar with Olympians.

Old Orpheus sang in Hades
to bring back unbroken flesh;
but it took gettin' ripped with maenads
to get him back to Eurydice.

And Jesus Christ was undivided
before he hung up on the cross
where he got rent all into pieces,
God and Son and Holy ghost.

So six months ain't no sentence
and a year is not no time,
long as I ain't in Angola
stayin' whole and gettin' dry.

Death will break you up in pieces,
but only after you're in the soil
where you drink Lethe's bland water
with the millions who stayed whole.

Now if I had me a million dollars,
just one million for my own,
I'd buy up old Angola,
plow the ground and plant a farm.

I'd grow grapes for Dionysus,
cypresses for Orpheus,
and a slew of sturdy Cross trees
to hold up Lawd Jesus.

So give me water when I'm thirsty,
mix that water with some wine:
let it break my blood and body up
and leave me feelin' fine.

Give me time when I get sickly,
if I start rottin' on this road.
Keep me whole enough to shatter,
Lawd, 'fore I'm buried in the loam.

And if you see me knocked out loaded,
forget about my old drunk hide.
I'm just tearin' myself up
'fore I'm swallowed by the ground.

JOHN HENRY

When I was just a little baby boy
you could hold me on the palm of your hand.
But I grew hard as bone
and as big as mountain stone
and became the greatest steel drivin' man.

With my nine-pound hammer I can terrify the gods
when I break the earth foundations of their sky.
If I came to Olympus
I'd crush them crags right down to dust
or I'd lay down my hammer and I'd die.

My steel makes mountains tremble like the dying of a god,
and sparks explode like thorns around my head.
I just squint and hammer on
to clear the way and prove I'm strong
to break the rocks where fires of gods are fed.

I ain't the first of mortals to drive steel into the earth
and uncover what men weren't meant to see;
there was plenty came before
and they'll keep on bein' more
long as stone stands for tunneling between.

Prometheus stole that holy fire from heaven
'fore man had smelted steel for him to drive.
He climbed Olympus' rocks
and snuck that flame into a stalk
so he could bring it down for men to feel divine.

Zeus hung him on the rocks he'd struggled up on
and an eagle ate his liver every day.
Though his guts got ripped apart,
he had seen the face of god
and his chains smiled in the fires that he had made.

Now men have made a steam drill to dig tunnels
to keep from bein' buried by the rocks;
but like Prometheus felt pain
when he was chewed up on his chain
I still hammer, breathin' stone, to face the gods.

They lined me up against that ol' steam hammer,
said *Let's see if you can lick what won't get tired.*
With my hammer at my side
I vowed I'd win or I would die
and I struck that mountain, bathing in its fire.

So here I fall among the sparks and rubble
three full feet ahead of that machine.
A man ain't nothin' but a man
and now my eyes are getting dim;
this hammer's gonna be the death of me.

But Lawd God I'm gonna swing this nine-pound hammer
'til you come and stop this hammerin' heart of mine.
Let me see Prometheus' fire
shine around me as I die
and grin at you as I become divine.

And Lawd let me break one final tunnel
that leads where real steel drivin' men all go
when they dare to face the gods
like Jesus driven to his cross,
and learn what men were never meant to know.

They'll bury me beside this broken mountain's stones
so my bones can hear the trains go rumblin' by.
They'll say *He breathed his last*
swingin' a hammer hard and fast:
yonder lies a real steel drivin' man.

LEADBELLY

"There ain't no doctor, in all the lan'
Can cure the fever of a convict man"

— Huddie William Leadbetter, *Midnight Special*

Well you wake up every mornin'
and you hear the ding-dong ring;
go marchin' to the table
and see the same damn thing:
all on the same ole table
a knife, a fork, and pan
like a branch of pomegranates
beyond Tantalus' hands.

As they make you sit and eat it,
you know he felt this way
when he reached up for them boughs
and they kept pullin' away;
or when he tried to drink the water
always just below his chin,
cause y'all both can't pick your food
when your stomach's rumblin'.

It's the hunger, not the eatin',
that gets in a convict's guts
and keeps'em aching for the limbs
or some finger-lickin' stuff;
like the apple up in Eden
or the gall up on the Cross,
or the feast set for divinities
that busted Tanatalus.

That's the closest man has gotten
to gettin' even with the gods
for givin' us the appetites
a lifetime couldn't calm.
When that king served human flesh,
those gods tasted the meat
of the convict men of earth
whose hunger feeds the deities.

So they cursed him to be hungry
in his lush infernal grove,
and even though he'll ache forever
it ain't much different here above.
'Cause we all eat prison grub,
hungry for what's cooked beyond
where you never feel them pangs
that keep you calling out to god.

Like when Rosie come to see me
in the heat of last July,
how she snuck me a little coffee,
and a slice of her sweet pie.
But she couldn't bring me nuthin'
to calm my belly none;
gave me damn near everythin'
'cept that jailhouse key I want.

So every night I finish dinner,
shuffle back into my cell.
The lights go out and I lay down,
wondrin' what they serve in hell.
Then I hear that well-known rumble,
like the one from my insides,
and the train that comes at midnight
turns the corner, lit up bright.

The light becomes a pomegranate
hung above the lake of night
and I'm Tantalus for a moment
as I reach to take a bite.
But the fruit just fades away
and the pond sinks at my feet
and I fall asleep another night,
hungry for eternity.

But let the Midnight Special
shine her light on me
like the fruit the gods hold up
that makes them live in my belly.

CASEY JONES

Of all the rounders on the rails,
they trust me with the Southbound mail.
I climb in the cab, my orders in hand,
to take a trip to the Promised Land.

Whenever I am at the wheel
I think about how Icarus fell
and smell the coal that drives my train
melt like the wax that clipped his wings.

He got to fly up near the sun
until the heat left him undone.
He soared like no man before or since,
despite the words of Daedalus.

The father flew on, not knowing why
the son destroyed what made him fly:
that marrowed urge to outstrip old men
on the waxen wings that carried them.

My coal was mined from Icarus' wax;
he had the sun and I have these tracks,
the limits that our father's mapped
like metered lines we must surpass.

So I mull how he flew too high
and burned his fathers sound design;
like someone singing an old train song
and making the words and rhyme all wrong.

Through South Memphis yards I'm on the fly,
fireman says I've got a white-eye.
But I keep the engine hot as the sun
the coal keeps burnin', the train flies on.

I tell the fireman not to fret,
keep the fire door knockin', don't give up yet,
'cause I'm going to run till we leave these rails
or make it on time with the Southbound mail.

I speed along the steel-wrought roads
monotonous as the white of bones
to see if I can break these lines
old men left me to stay inside.

'Cause that's what makes it worth the fall:
to melt that ancient wax and coal
and burn, eternal engineer
whose crash rings in creators' ears.

So the fireman jumps but I stay on
to leave those tracks where no one's gone
and fly like Icarus just one time
past where fathers put down their lines.

JOE MCKENNEDY

— St. James Infirmary

I went down to St. James Infirmary
and saw my baby there.
She was stretched out cold as Hector
when Achilles stripped him bare.

The dead harden into marble
that the quick build altars from
to the gods of stone and memory
that we all will soon become.

Achilles carved the corpse of Hector
on them juttin' Trojan stones
like a priest who knows the rituals
for burnin' fat-wrapped bones.

Priam must have wanted whiskey
as he watched up on the walls
like me here drinkin' bourbon
wondrin' where my baby's gone.

But let her go, let her go, God bless her,
wherever she may be.
She's stone and memory on this table,
but my song drags her in back of me

like Hector dragged behind Achilles,
leaving men to hymn his death:
how Achilles made an altar
from those broken bits of flesh.

'Cause stone and memory keep the gods
in their rock temples and rites,
just as bones of dead men petrify
in earth, leaving relics of their lives.

I feel the pain of Priam
begging for his broken son.
He had to see with granite eyes
to grasp what Hector had become.

And then he drank with Hector's killer
knowing his son's flesh had touched a Muse
who'd make'em into gods in songs,
like my St. James Infirmary Blues.

So sixteen coal black horses
to pull that rubber-tied hack;
like Hector bouncin' behind Achilles,
she's gone; only my song can bring her back.

KAWLIGA

Kawliga was a wooden Indian
standin' by the door.
He fell in love with the Indian maiden
over in the antique store.
Their timbered hearts both wanted just one day
to feel the flesh that blossomed in the Tree.

Trunks can grow from lovers' chests,
branch out into their veins;
roots take hold below the limbs
in the soil where man was made:
like Philemon and Baucis intertwined,
whose love made Zeus turn them to oak and lime.

Those two grew ripe on moldy earth,
fermented in their veins;
bruised and spoiled, skin shriveled up,
their limbs doomed to ruin.
They would have entered earth and turned to mud,
but their flesh was overgrown by love's heartwood.

Kawliga wears his Sunday feathers
and holds his tomahawk.
The maiden wears her beads and braids
and hopes someday he'll talk.
But they should know their love is now divine
since they're already turned to knotty pine.

She'll never feel the birthing pangs
or know a widow's loss.
His chiseled chest and arms won't sag,
he won't rot in a pine box.
They'll never know the slipping of the flesh
that made man fall like apples into death.

The love that cast us from the grove
was planted in our mouths.
That first fruit made us arch our backs,
stretch limbs in forbidden boughs.
A taste doomed us to rot but left those seeds,
sowed in our chests God's knowledge of the trees.

Like Philemon and Baucis
stand Kawliga and his maid
all turned to wood of Eden's growth,
no skin to fall away.
Soft as loam, we love while we still breathe
and hope one day to enter earth as trees.

FRANKIE AND JOHNNY

Me and Frankie were sweethearts,
Lord, how we did love.
Even Jason and Medea
didn't have nothin' on us.
I was her man;
I wouldn't do her wrong.

But love's a flesh-starved dragon
who waits under a tree
until you find a woman
to help you make him sleep.
And you'll be her man
to keep that serpent calm.

She'll help you get the glistenin' skins
her daddy don't want stole,
the golden fleece gods gave him
that you want for your own
from off the branch
like an apple hung.

She'll spend a hundred dollars
to buy you some new clothes.
She'd chop up her own brother
and toss his butchered bones
at her old man
to keep you safe from harm.

And you'll forget that dragon
whose breath burned in your gut
and you'll kiss her while you're fleein',
hold her hands still wet with blood.
Cause you're her man,
and she can do no wrong.

But a serpent don't stay sleepin'
'cause he always needs to eat,
and when your girl's no longer charmin',
he'll crawl off to find warm meat.
You can hear his scales
whenever you're alone.

And then you'll clean forget her
'cause you feel that dragon's coils
twistin' up around your thighs
as you kiss on some new girl
with a golden skin
to lay that monster down.

But she'll walk to the corner,
like my Frankie went for beer,
and she'll ask the old bartender
Has my lovin' man been here?
Then she'll go mad,
just like Medea done.

She'll walk down to that brothel,
forty-four under her shirt
lethal as that fiery mantle
that devoured Jason's flirt
and her poor old man,
rippin' skin from bone.

She'll find you with your lover,
wish she'd left you to that snake,
then root-a-toot that gal will shoot
and send you to your grave,
or kill your two young sons
and leave you all alone.

Then it's a rubber-tired buggy
to take you to your tomb,
and a chariot drawn by serpents
to fly her far from you
and leave you with the skin
that leads the dragon on.

IRENE

Last Saturday night I got married,
me and my wife settled down.
Now she's flown just like Medea
who left Jason spell-bound .

Sometimes I live in the country,
sometimes I live in the town;
but since my girl's a false charmer
I'll go jump in the river and drown.

A pretty witch will make you love her,
make the flesh-starved dragon sleep
that guards the fleece hung on the branch
like an apple in a tree.

She'll get them skins dad don't want stolen
then help you make your getaway
and you'll forget about that serpent
only she can keep at bay.

Like when Irene's mother told me
that her daughter was too young
and I remembered how Medea
tricked her man like Irene done.

'Cause Jason watched his sweet-lipped lover
tear her brother limb from limb
and toss the still warm bleedin' parts
in a wake of father's screams.

But by then you've been bewitched
same as that dragon by the tree
and you'll wish it would've killed you
'fore you let her help you flee.

Stop your ramblin', stop your gamblin'
stop runnin' with tongue-talkin' gals.
Go home to your wife and family;
don't get caught in witches spells.

Cause you can't trust girls who trick you,
make you love them with a lie,
anymore than dragon-charmers
who dismember family.

And you can't split although you want it
cause she'll never let you leave
as long as she controls that viper
sleepin' back under the tree.

Try and go and she will wake it,
kill your wife and both your sons,
then flee in a chariot of fire
dragged behind that woke dragon.

I love Irene, God knows I do,
but I remember witches lie.
And if Irene's a Medea,
I'll take morphine and die.

Goodnight Irene, you Medea,
goodnight you serpent queen.
Your spells once calmed my dragons,
but now they burn me in my dreams.

LITTLE LIZA JANE

I got a girl in love with me,
Little Liza Jane.
She's patient as Penelope
with her driftin' man.

There's Ithacas in both the eyes
of Little Liza Jane.
They call me back home every time
I get in wine-dark straits.

Them seas that wrecked Odysseus
roll in every man.
They swell in depths down in his chest
and surge in every gland.

So I'm gonna throw these dice away
to make Little Liza mine;
toss'em till they reach Circe
lurkin' on her isle.

'Cause wine will turn men into hogs
who root in mud for swill
that's tossed to them by voodoo broads
so they'll forget home meals.

That bumble bee be out for sips
but I'm done with the booze.
It takes my sweetmeats from Jane's lips
and keeps me from my house.

I'm sick of smoke and dancin' girls
who sing them siren songs
that lure men to their hidden shoals
and swallow up their bones.

I'll leave the dope to gigolos
to waste away alone
like the drunken Lotus-Eaters dozed
when Odysseus sailed home.

Give me my house in the Seventh Ward
on an inlet of the sea
where waves still wash from ancient shores
and break inside of me.

Never more from you I'll roam,
Little Liza Jane.
Best place to be is home sweet home
where men can't wash away.

PART 5—TAXONOMIES

THE ELEPHANT GRAVES

Elephants know a macadam of bone,
cracked hips, shin shards, old tusks, and skulls,
gravel of pachyderms whose blood seeps through
in streams the young ones drink and spray at flies.
This road cuts through their marrow like jackal's teeth
and winds in their huge heads like memory.

They always find this path by memory
bequeathed to them by something in their bones.
It grows in girth and hardens with their long teeth.
They reach its end when death seeps in their skulls,
where the road will soon extend with help from flies
who chew the dead to asphalt when they're through.

No such gravel road passes through
the world of man, who buries memory
under stones to keep away the flies.
He never cuts his feet on kindred bone
or passes through the tunnels of a skull.
His only shards of jaw are lost teeth.

But death still sticks like cartilage in his teeth,
gristle he won't feel till the meal's done.
And as his last breath rattles in his skull,
he'll wish he had an elephant's memory,
two tusks, a trunk to curl on ancient bone,
and feel inside his snout the way flesh flies.

Instead his eyes sputter like fireflies,
fear leeches in gasps between clenched teeth,
and muscles tighten down his bent backbone.
It's night and he does not know a way through,
no road passed down through marrow and memory
that leads where he can empty out his skull.

What fills the dumb elephant's huge skull
that's not in man's who made hard metal fly,
made God, and keeps Him alive in memory?
What's in the tusks that's not in wisdom teeth
that keeps men from finding roads through
death, where elephants walk macadams of bone?
Perhaps the memory weighs down our skulls,
too hard for human bone and fearful eyes.
The gums of death, our teeth cannot cut through.

THE MINOANS OF ANGOLA

After two days of rain the earth turns
to mud, the clay kind that sticks to you
like sinews to bone or the ribs
they sell in stalls outside the gates.
Its hard to grip this lathered ground
that ripples in folds of brown and red
like the shoulders and flanks of bulls.

You come to watch a man bare-back on earth-
toned bulls that lurch like the hills in mudslides
when God divided earth and sea.
The rider has to hold for eight full counts
the beast that breathed before him.
So on those architectonic backs of mud-
caked flesh, man and what came first are one,
momentary minotaurs, bull gods of creation.

You think about the Minoans
as the rider falls beneath the horns and hooves.
He staggers back behind the chutes
and stands devoured by the bull-
tinged mud, like those Athenian youths
sentenced to be thrown in Minos' maze.
Eight seconds in the bull-god's maw
fused them in those pre-human thighs.

The rodeo is a labyrinth
of seats, chutes, gates, and paths
around the rutted arena floor.
You watch the sentenced men on earth
that quakes and roils where bulls stomp.
They make you cringe at the thought:
cracked ribs, muddy hooves that bolt flesh.

Somewhere back below the stands
Herefords and Brahmas paw
the earth with bulging thighs.

POLYNEICES

A strong north wind and falling tides bare the earth
under Lake Pontchartrain where days ago the mullets schooled.
Its strange to see the surface blown away like skirts
in gusty games of blind man's bluff, instants
when we glimpse the covered world below and slow our chase.

Beyond its sandbar, the lake rarely shows its bottom
so far out, where children now run on the flats.
When what's below uncovers and bares
the soil we'd never see without this low tide,
we can feel between our toes the mud that moves in us.

Beneath in current furrows lie the dying clams,
their shells small mausoleums where what should be
below remains above like tombs next to interstates.
It smells vaguely familiar, the salt of skin
in naked shoals and these gasping small deaths.

Some lie partly covered in the exposed mud
waiting for small Antigones to bury them
in the silt of their birth, the sediment of their decay.
This painful beauty, uncovered earth in tides,
digs into you like clams as children dig their holes.

After two calm days the lake is back to normal,
and only pilings jut like thighs from ruffled sheets
to hint that there is ground below the modest,
winking waves that gouge our eyes like Oedipus,
leave us blind to things that move below the surface.

EPITHALAMION

– For Emily

Two bayous become a lake in this shoal mud,
shallow as shut eyes where the bottom can only be
felt in the dark, like breaths. Their mouths open and meet
the broad eternity of tides, merging in beds

of turtle grass. We see ourselves in the water,
swells folding always into each other to create
the shore, where spartina shimmers as we wade
through shallows, hazel eyes reflecting September.

The brackish tide tastes of warm skin, and your lips
feel the memory of rain in this ancient union
of Gulf salt and fresh streams. Our legs move as the waves' rhythms
surge through us and spend themselves in the ebbs

      that feed the shrimp and crabs in this fertile silt. We rest
      on the beach, aglow in the soft Fall sun, caressed

      like sea-glass by the breeze. I reach for you as an egret
      strides, rising from these waters he has known since the nest

on the sandbar where he feeds. Your eyes shine; salt-marsh mallows
violet and white in the green oyster grass
tremble like reason before the breath of the vast
afternoon, whose gusts play in your hair. Between us time goes

slow as the growth and erosion of shores. I kneel in the sand
and smell the age of an estuary rise around us.
The day dissolves in the shimmering of joined bodies
of water between the sky and earth and our hands,

and I ask you to become a lake with me,
to merge our headwatered hearts with the eternal
depth of salt that rises in springs, falls in neaps,
and reflects us on the mirror of these shoals.

AN OAK

— For Jack William

Slender as a sapling, your neck bears a crown of new growth,
oak-brown hair layered in whorls like rings of trees.
Inside an acorn, unsprung roots and boughs
share the kindred genesis that drives synapses

to sprout from this stem seeded in your mother's womb.
Curls drape like catkins around the knots of your ears
whose hollows hold your mind's sapwood and phloem,
neurons spreading their branches. The vertebrae of years

will lengthen your trunk and limbs, make this infant skin
rough as bark, bearded like mine with the moss of age.
And when time has turned my hair the grey of dying
cypresses, I will see my life in this foliage

born from our old loam, evergreen, and our blood
running in the veins of your heartwood.